Sold!

A Complete Guide for Selling Your Home

Cheryl Waller, MBA

ISBN: 9798396195110

TABLE OF CONTENTS

SETTING GOALS AND OBJECTIVES FOR SELLING

Selling a home is a significant endeavor that involves careful planning, strategic decision-making, and effective execution. Whether you're a seasoned homeowner or a first-time seller, it is crucial to approach the process with clear goals and well-defined objectives. Setting goals and objectives not only provides a sense of direction but also helps you stay focused, organized, and motivated throughout the selling journey.

In this chapter, we will delve into the essential aspects of setting goals and objectives when selling your home. We will explore the importance of establishing realistic and measurable targets that align with your financial, logistical, and personal aspirations. By taking the time to articulate your goals, you'll be able to create a roadmap that guides your actions, facilitates effective communication with real estate professionals, and maximizes your chances of achieving a successful sale.

To begin, we'll discuss the primary reasons why setting goals and objectives is crucial in the home-selling process. By understanding the benefits, you'll gain a clearer perspective on how goal-setting can empower you as a seller. We will then delve into the different types of goals you may consider, including financial goals, timeline goals, and property-specific goals, among others. Each type of goal serves a specific purpose and helps you prioritize and manage your selling process effectively.

Moreover, this chapter will provide you with practical tips and strategies for setting realistic goals. We will explore how to conduct market research, analyze comparable properties, and assess your home's unique selling points to determine an appropriate listing price and target sales figure. Additionally, we will discuss the significance of establishing a timeline and how it influences your objectives, such as closing dates, moving plans, and any time-sensitive considerations.

Furthermore, we will emphasize the importance of collaboration and communication with your real estate agent or any professionals involved in the selling process. Effective dialogue ensures that your goals and objectives are aligned with their expertise and capabilities, facilitating a smooth and successful partnership. We will offer guidance on how to effectively communicate your goals, listen to their recommendations, and work together to optimize your chances of achieving a favorable outcome.

Lastly, we will highlight the role of flexibility and adaptability in goal-setting. Selling a home can be a dynamic process with unexpected twists and turns. By remaining open to adjusting your goals and objectives as needed, you can respond to market fluctuations, buyer feedback, and changing circumstances, while still staying focused on your ultimate objective of selling your home at the best possible terms.

Throughout this chapter, we aim to equip you with the knowledge and insights necessary to set meaningful goals and objectives for selling your home. By investing time and effort into this critical phase, you will enhance your overall selling experience and increase the likelihood of a successful and satisfying outcome. So, let's dive in and embark on this exciting journey toward achieving your home-selling goals.

Setting Goals and Objectives When Selling Your Home

When it comes to selling your home, setting clear goals and objectives is a fundamental step in ensuring a smooth and successful process. By establishing concrete targets, you provide yourself with a roadmap that guides your decision-making, keeps you focused, and maximizes your chances of achieving a favorable outcome.

First and foremost, setting goals and objectives provides you with a sense of direction. It allows you to clarify what you hope to achieve through the sale of your home. Are you looking to maximize profit, sell quickly, or find a buyer who appreciates the unique features of your property? Defining your goals helps you prioritize and make informed choices throughout the selling journey.

Moreover, well-defined goals enable you to stay organized. They provide a framework for planning and executing the necessary tasks, such as staging, marketing, and negotiating. With clear objectives in mind, you can create a timeline and checklist to ensure that you address all the essential aspects of the selling process, from preparing your home for listing to finalizing the sale.

Setting goals also helps you stay motivated. Selling a home can be a complex and occasionally stressful endeavor. However, when you have specific targets to work towards, it becomes easier to stay focused and overcome challenges along the way. Goals provide a sense of purpose and can serve as a source of inspiration during times when the process feels overwhelming.

To effectively set goals and objectives, consider various factors. Financial goals are often a top priority, determining how much profit you aim to make or how much you can afford to invest in repairs or renovations. Timeline goals help establish a realistic timeframe for selling your home, considering external factors like market conditions and personal circumstances. Property-specific goals focus on showcasing your home's unique features and attracting the right buyers.

It's important to collaborate with a trusted real estate agent or professional who can help you set realistic goals and guide you through the process. Their expertise and market knowledge can provide valuable insights when determining achievable targets and developing a strategic approach to selling your home.

In conclusion, setting goals and objectives when selling your home is essential for a successful and satisfying experience. By defining your goals, staying organized, and seeking professional guidance, you increase your chances of achieving your desired outcomes, whether it be a profitable sale, a quick transaction, or finding the perfect buyer who appreciates your property. So take the time to set your goals, and embark on your home-selling journey with confidence.

Conducting Market Research

Market research plays a vital role in the process of selling your home. It provides valuable insights into the current real estate market, helps you determine an appropriate listing price, and enables you to make informed decisions throughout the selling process. By conducting thorough market research, you increase your chances of attracting qualified buyers and achieving a successful sale.

One of the primary reasons to conduct market research is to gain a comprehensive understanding of the local real estate market. This includes analyzing recent sales data, studying trends, and examining the supply and demand dynamics in your area. By examining comparable properties that have recently sold or are currently on the market, you can gauge the market's response and make informed pricing decisions.

When conducting market research, it's important to consider various factors that influence property values. These factors may include location, property size, amenities, condition, and recent upgrades or renovations. By evaluating how similar properties are priced and perceived in the market, you can determine a competitive listing price that reflects the value of your home.

In addition to pricing, market research helps you understand buyer preferences and expectations. By identifying the target market for your property, you can tailor your marketing efforts to appeal to potential buyers. For example, if your home is located in a family-friendly neighborhood, you may highlight nearby schools and parks in your marketing materials. Understanding the desires and needs of potential buyers allows you to position your home effectively and attract qualified leads.

Moreover, market research provides insights into market conditions and trends. Real estate markets can fluctuate, and it's crucial to stay informed about any shifts that may impact your selling strategy. For instance, understanding whether it's a buyer's or seller's market can influence your negotiation approach and timeline goals.

To conduct effective market research, it's beneficial to collaborate with a knowledgeable real estate agent or utilize online resources and local data. Real estate professionals have access to industry databases, market reports, and historical data that can offer a comprehensive view of the market. They can also provide expert analysis and guidance based on their experience and understanding of current market trends.

In conclusion, market research is a crucial step when selling your home. By examining market conditions, analyzing comparable properties, and understanding buyer preferences, you can set an appropriate listing price, position your property effectively, and make informed decisions throughout the selling process. The insights gained from market research will empower you as a seller and increase your chances of achieving a successful and satisfactory sale.

Analyzing Comparable Properties

Analyzing comparable properties, also known as comps, is a critical component of conducting market research when selling your home. Comparables are properties that are similar to yours in terms of location, size, features, and condition, and they serve as a benchmark for determining the value of your home in the current real estate market. By carefully evaluating and comparing these properties, you can make informed pricing decisions and position your home effectively to attract potential buyers.

When analyzing comparable properties, consider the following factors:

- Location: Start by looking for properties in the same neighborhood or nearby areas. Location plays a significant role in determining property values, as amenities, school districts, proximity to transportation, and neighborhood desirability can all impact the price.

- Size and Layout: Compare the size and layout of your home to the comps. Consider factors such as the number of bedrooms, bathrooms, square footage, and any unique features or layout characteristics. Adjustments may be necessary if your home differs significantly in size or layout from the comparable properties.

- Condition and Upgrades: Assess the overall condition of the comparable properties, including any renovations or upgrades they may have undergone. A property in better condition or with desirable upgrades may command a higher price. Conversely, if your home requires repairs or updates, you may need to adjust the price accordingly.

- Recent Sales: Look at the recent sales data of comparable properties that have recently sold. Pay attention to the sale prices and how long the properties were on the market. This information can give you a sense of the market activity and help you gauge buyer interest.

- Active Listings: Review the properties that are currently listed for sale and similar to yours. Analyze their listing prices, features, and time on the market. This will give you a sense of the competition your home will face and help you determine a competitive listing price.

When analyzing comparable properties, it's essential to be objective and consider the data objectively. While emotions may be attached to your home, it's crucial to look at the market value and buyer perception realistically. Working with a trusted real estate agent can be beneficial, as they have access to comprehensive market data and can provide expert guidance in analyzing and interpreting comparable properties.

By conducting a thorough analysis of comparable properties, you can determine a fair and competitive listing price for your home. This will increase your chances of attracting potential buyers, generating interest, and ultimately achieving a successful sale within a reasonable timeframe.

Assessing Your Home's Unique Selling Points

When selling your home, understanding and effectively showcasing its unique selling points is crucial in capturing the attention of potential buyers and maximizing its market appeal. These unique features and characteristics set your home apart from others on the market, making it stand out and potentially influencing buyers' purchasing decisions. By assessing and highlighting these selling points, you can position your home to attract the right buyers and potentially command a higher selling price.

Here are some steps to assess your home's unique selling points:

Take an objective perspective: Step back and try to view your home through the eyes of a potential buyer. This allows you to identify its standout features without personal bias. Consider both the interior and exterior aspects of your home, including architectural details, layout, landscaping, and any distinctive elements that could make a lasting impression.

Consider location advantages: Evaluate your home's location and proximity to amenities, schools, parks, shopping centers, public transportation, and other desirable features. A convenient location can be a significant selling point for buyers, so make sure to emphasize its benefits.

Evaluate architectural and design elements: Assess the architectural style and design elements of your home. Unique architectural features like vaulted ceilings, custom molding, or large windows can add value and attract buyers. Additionally, consider interior design elements such as open floor plans, modern upgrades, or custom finishes that set your home apart.

Highlight functional features: Identify any functional features that enhance the livability and convenience of your home. This can include features like a well-designed kitchen, ample storage space, energy-efficient appliances, smart home technology, or a well-maintained HVAC system. These features can be compelling selling points for buyers seeking practicality and efficiency.

Showcase outdoor spaces: If your home has appealing outdoor areas, such as a well-landscaped yard, a deck, patio, or a swimming pool, make sure to showcase them. Well-maintained and inviting outdoor spaces can significantly enhance your home's market appeal, particularly for buyers who value outdoor living and entertainment options.

Consider unique neighborhood attributes: Evaluate any unique attributes of your neighborhood that may be appealing to buyers. These could include a sense of community, nearby parks or recreational areas, low crime rates, or access to sought-after school districts. Highlighting these neighborhood features can be influential in attracting the right buyers.

Once you've identified your home's unique selling points, it's important to effectively showcase them in your marketing materials and during home showings. Utilize high-quality photographs, well-crafted descriptions, and virtual tours to highlight these features. Additionally, communicate with your real estate agent to ensure they understand and can effectively communicate these selling points to potential buyers.

By assessing and emphasizing your home's unique selling points, you can create a compelling narrative that resonates with buyers. This can lead to increased buyer interest, quicker sale times, and potentially a higher selling price. Remember to capitalize on what makes your home special and position it as a desirable and unique property in the market.

Establishing A Timeline

When selling your home, establishing a timeline is essential for keeping the selling process organized, setting realistic expectations, and ensuring a smooth transition to your next home. A well-planned timeline helps you stay on track, meet important milestones, and effectively coordinate various tasks and activities associated with selling your home. Here are key steps to consider when establishing a timeline:

- Preparing your home for sale: Determine the timeframe needed to prepare your home for listing. This may involve decluttering, deep cleaning, making necessary repairs or renovations, and staging the property. Consider the condition of your home and the scope of work required to present it in the best possible light. Set a reasonable timeline that allows for ample preparation without unnecessary delays.

- Selecting a real estate agent: Take into account the time required to research, interview, and select a reputable real estate agent. It's important to find an agent who understands your goals, has a proven track record, and is knowledgeable about your local market. Allow sufficient time to discuss your selling objectives, review marketing strategies, and establish a solid working relationship with your chosen agent.

- Pricing and marketing strategy: Collaborate with your real estate agent to determine an appropriate listing price based on market research, comparable properties, and your goals. Discuss the marketing strategy, including professional photography, virtual tours, open houses, and online listings. Allocate time for the development and implementation of a comprehensive marketing plan to attract potential buyers.

- Showings and negotiations: Consider the time needed for showings and potential negotiations with buyers. Be flexible with scheduling showings and allow adequate time for potential buyers to visit your home. Factor in the time required to review offers, negotiate terms, and potentially counteroffer or accept an offer. Work closely with your real estate agent to navigate this stage efficiently.

- Closing and moving: Anticipate the timeline for the closing process, including inspections, appraisals, and the completion of required paperwork. Coordinate with the buyer, their agent, and your real estate agent to ensure a smooth closing process. Additionally, allocate time for packing, coordinating movers, and transitioning to your new home. Depending on your circumstances, this timeline may vary.

Throughout the timeline, it's crucial to remain flexible and adaptable to unexpected circumstances or changes in market conditions. While establishing a timeline is important, be prepared for adjustments and be responsive to feedback from your real estate agent and potential buyers.

Remember to communicate regularly with your real estate agent to stay informed and aligned with the timeline. They can provide guidance, updates, and help keep the process on track.

By establishing a well-thought-out timeline, you can effectively manage the selling process, reduce stress, and increase the likelihood of a successful sale within your desired timeframe.

Collaboration And Communication

When selling your home, effective collaboration and communication with your real estate agent or any professionals involved in the selling process are essential for a successful and smooth experience. Open and transparent communication fosters a strong working relationship, ensures alignment of goals and expectations, and maximizes the expertise and support you receive throughout the selling journey. Here are key aspects to consider when collaborating with your real estate agent or other professionals:

Establish clear objectives: Clearly communicate your goals, priorities, and timeline to your real estate agent or professionals. This includes your desired sale price, desired timeline for selling, and any specific preferences or concerns you have. By setting clear objectives from the beginning, you establish a foundation for effective collaboration.

Regular communication: Maintain regular and open lines of communication with your real estate agent or professionals. This includes scheduled check-ins, updates on market activity, feedback from showings, and discussions about marketing strategies or adjustments. Regular communication ensures that you are informed and involved throughout the selling process.

Share information openly: Provide relevant information about your property, its history, and any unique features or selling points. This allows your real estate agent to craft compelling marketing materials and effectively promote your home to potential buyers. Be open and honest about any known issues or repairs, as transparency builds trust and avoids surprises during the transaction.

Seek professional guidance: Your real estate agent or professionals are valuable resources with extensive knowledge and experience. Be open to their guidance and advice regarding pricing strategies, staging suggestions, marketing techniques, and negotiation tactics. Trust their expertise and be receptive to their recommendations.

Collaborate on marketing efforts: Work closely with your real estate agent or professionals to develop and execute a comprehensive marketing plan. This may include professional photography, virtual tours, online listings, open houses, and targeted marketing campaigns. Provide input and feedback on marketing materials and strategies to ensure they align with your vision and attract the right buyers.

Review offers and negotiate: Collaborate closely with your real estate agent during the offer review and negotiation process. Discuss the terms, conditions, and any counteroffers or concessions you may consider. Your agent's expertise in negotiating on your behalf can help you achieve your desired outcome.

Stay responsive and adaptable: Be prompt in responding to communication from your real estate agent or professionals. Timely responses facilitate efficient decision-making and keep the selling process moving forward. Additionally, be open to adapting your strategies or adjusting your expectations based on market feedback or changing circumstances.

Remember that collaboration and communication are a two-way street. Actively listen to the advice and insights of your real estate agent or professionals and provide feedback when necessary. A collaborative approach creates a productive and harmonious working relationship, leading to a successful sale and a positive overall experience.

By fostering effective collaboration and communication with your real estate agent or professionals, you can leverage their expertise, align your efforts, and navigate the selling process with confidence and efficiency. Together, you can work towards achieving your selling goals and ensuring a satisfactory outcome.

PREPARING YOUR HOME FOR SALE: STAGING AND PRESENTATION

Preparing your home for sale is a crucial step in attracting potential buyers, maximizing its market appeal, and ultimately achieving a successful and profitable sale. In this chapter, we will delve into the art of staging and presentation, exploring effective strategies and techniques to transform your home into an irresistible and welcoming space that captivates buyers' attention.

In today's competitive real estate market, where first impressions matter more than ever, staging plays a vital role in showcasing your home's unique features, optimizing its visual appeal, and helping buyers envision themselves living in the space. By carefully considering every aspect of your home's presentation, from decluttering and organizing to enhancing curb appeal and creating inviting interiors, you can create an environment that resonates with potential buyers and sets your home apart from the competition.

This chapter will guide you through the process of preparing your home for sale, starting with an assessment of your property's strengths and areas for improvement. We will explore how to effectively declutter and depersonalize your home, allowing buyers to envision their own belongings in the space. Additionally, we will discuss the importance of thorough cleaning, minor repairs, and freshening up the overall appearance of your home.

Moreover, staging goes beyond mere tidiness and cleanliness. We will delve into the art of interior design and arranging furniture and décor to highlight the best features of each room, create a sense of flow and harmony, and evoke a welcoming atmosphere. From strategic furniture placement to the use of neutral color palettes and tasteful accessories, we will provide insights and practical tips to transform your home into a visually appealing and inviting haven.

Furthermore, this chapter will address the significance of curb appeal in creating a positive first impression. We will explore ways to enhance your home's exterior, from landscaping and maintenance to improving the façade, entryway, and outdoor living areas. By maximizing curb appeal, you can entice potential buyers and pique their curiosity to explore the rest of your property.

Throughout this chapter, we will emphasize the importance of balancing personal touches with broad market appeal. While it's crucial to create a neutral and inviting environment, we will guide you on how to infuse subtle elements that make your home feel warm and lived-in, without overwhelming buyers with excessive personalization.

By investing time and effort into staging and presentation, you can elevate your home's desirability, create a memorable impression, and ultimately increase its market value. So, let's embark on this journey of transforming your home into a captivating showpiece that captures the hearts of potential buyers.

An Assessment of Your Property

Before putting your home on the market, conducting a thorough assessment of your property's strengths and areas for improvement is a crucial step in preparing for a successful sale. Understanding the unique features that make your home desirable to potential buyers, as well as identifying any weaknesses or areas that may need attention, allows you to strategically position your property and maximize its market appeal. In this section, we will explore how to assess your property objectively, highlighting its strengths and determining areas that could benefit from improvement.

To begin the assessment, take a step back and approach your home with a fresh perspective. Look at it through the eyes of a potential buyer, considering what would make them fall in love with the property. Start by identifying the strengths and standout features that set your home apart from others on the market. These may include:

- Location: Assess the advantages of your home's location, such as proximity to schools, parks, shopping centers, or public transportation. Highlight any unique neighborhood attributes that potential buyers may find appealing.

- Architectural Features: Evaluate the architectural elements that contribute to the overall appeal of your home. This could include distinctive design elements, a well-maintained exterior, or charming historical details.

- Layout and Floor Plan: Consider the functionality and flow of your home's layout. A well-designed floor plan that maximizes space, offers natural light, and facilitates comfortable living can be a significant selling point.

- Upgrades and Renovations: Take note of any recent upgrades or renovations you have made to your home. These could include a modernized kitchen, updated bathrooms, energy-efficient appliances, or enhanced landscaping. Such improvements can attract buyers seeking move-in-ready properties.

- Outdoor Spaces: Assess your outdoor areas, such as a well-landscaped yard, a deck, patio, or a pool. Well-maintained outdoor spaces can greatly enhance your home's market appeal and provide additional living and entertainment options.

While identifying the strengths of your property is important, it is equally vital to recognize areas that may need improvement. These may include:

- Repairs and Maintenance: Identify any deferred maintenance or repairs that need attention. This could range from minor fixes like leaky faucets or peeling paint to more significant issues such as roof repairs or HVAC maintenance.

- Clutter and Organization: Evaluate the overall cleanliness and organization of your home. Decluttering and depersonalizing can create a more spacious and inviting environment for potential buyers.

- Neutralizing Personalization: Assess the extent of personalization in your home, including bold color schemes or personalized décor. Neutralizing these elements can help potential buyers envision themselves living in the space.

- Outdated or Dated Features: Take note of any outdated fixtures, appliances, or design elements that may benefit from updating. A more modern and timeless aesthetic can enhance your home's appeal.

By conducting a comprehensive assessment of your property's strengths and areas for improvement, you can develop a strategic plan to showcase its best features and address any weaknesses. Consider consulting with a trusted real estate agent who can provide an objective perspective and offer recommendations based on their market knowledge and expertise. With a well-rounded understanding of your property's condition and market potential, you can make informed decisions and take the necessary steps to prepare your home for a successful sale.

Decluttering And Organizing

One of the most impactful steps in preparing your home for sale is decluttering and organizing your living spaces. Clutter can make your home feel smaller, less appealing, and distract potential buyers from appreciating its true potential. By decluttering and organizing, you create a clean, spacious, and inviting environment that allows buyers to envision themselves living in the space. Here are key considerations and strategies for effectively decluttering and organizing your home:

- Start with a plan: Begin by developing a systematic plan of action. Break down your home into different areas or rooms and prioritize which spaces require the most attention. Establish a realistic timeline and set aside dedicated time for decluttering and organizing each area.

- Declutter ruthlessly: Be selective and ruthless when decluttering. Assess each item and ask yourself if it serves a practical purpose or if it holds sentimental value. Consider donating, selling, or disposing of items that no longer contribute to the functionality or aesthetic appeal of your home. This includes excess furniture, clothing, personal items, and knick-knacks.

- Clear out storage spaces: Pay close attention to storage areas such as closets, cabinets, and the garage. Potential buyers will open doors and look inside these spaces, so it's important to declutter and organize them. Remove unnecessary items, create a sense of space, and showcase the storage potential of each area.

- Organize and streamline: Once you have decluttered, focus on organizing the remaining items. Invest in storage solutions such as bins, baskets, and shelves to create a sense of order. Arrange items in a way that is visually pleasing and demonstrates the functionality of each space. Consider organizing items by category or purpose to make it easier for potential buyers to navigate.

- Minimize personalization: While decluttering and organizing, strive to create a neutral and depersonalized environment. Remove excessive personal items such as family photos, personal collections, and overly specific décor. This allows potential buyers to envision their own belongings in the space and creates a more universally appealing atmosphere.

- Enhance curb appeal: Declutter and organize outdoor areas as well. Clear away any unnecessary items, trim overgrown plants, and ensure walkways and entryways are clear and welcoming. First impressions matter, and a well-maintained exterior enhances the overall appeal of your home.

- Seek an outsider's perspective: Consider asking a friend or family member for their objective opinion on the decluttered and organized spaces. They may spot areas that need further attention or provide valuable feedback on the overall presentation.

Remember, decluttering and organizing is not just about tidying up—it's about creating a clean, open, and welcoming atmosphere that allows potential buyers to envision themselves living in your home. It's an opportunity to showcase the space and highlight its best features. By investing time and effort into this process, you increase the chances of attracting buyers, generating interest, and ultimately achieving a successful sale.

Staging Your Home

Staging your home is a powerful technique that can significantly enhance its appeal to potential buyers. By strategically arranging furniture, décor, and accessories, staging creates an inviting atmosphere that allows buyers to visualize themselves living in the space. It helps highlight your home's best features, maximizes its potential, and sets it apart from other properties on the market. In this section, we will explore key considerations and strategies for effectively staging your home:

- Depersonalize and neutralize: Start by depersonalizing your home to create a neutral canvas that appeals to a wide range of potential buyers. Remove personal photos, quirky artwork, and any items that may distract buyers from envisioning their own belongings in the space. Opt for neutral color schemes and décor that complements the overall aesthetic of your home.

- Highlight key features: Identify the unique selling points and architectural features of your home, and ensure they are showcased during the staging process. This could include a cozy fireplace, large windows with scenic views, or high ceilings. Arrange furniture and décor in a way that draws attention to these standout features and emphasizes their appeal.

- Create a sense of space: Use furniture placement to maximize the perception of space in each room.

Remove any unnecessary or oversized furniture that may make the space feel cramped. Arrange furniture to create an open flow, allowing potential buyers to move around easily and envision their own furniture arrangements.

- Accentuate natural light: Light is an essential aspect of staging. Open curtains and blinds to let in natural light and create a bright, inviting ambiance. Use mirrors strategically to reflect light and make rooms appear larger. Additionally, ensure that all light fixtures are clean and in working order to maximize illumination throughout your home.

- Add tasteful touches: Incorporate tasteful accessories and décor to enhance the overall aesthetic of your home. This may include fresh flowers, stylish throw pillows, and carefully selected artwork. However, be mindful of not overdoing it; a clutter-free and thoughtfully curated environment is key.

- Pay attention to details: Little details can make a big difference in the overall impression of your home. Ensure that each room is clean, tidy, and free of any visible wear and tear. Replace burned-out light bulbs, fix minor damages, and address any noticeable issues that may catch buyers' attention.

- Don't forget about curb appeal: The exterior of your home is the first thing potential buyers see, so make a positive impression from the moment they arrive. Ensure that the front yard is well-maintained, the entrance is inviting, and any outdoor spaces are staged to showcase their potential for relaxation or entertainment.

- Consider professional staging: If you feel overwhelmed or lack an eye for design, consider hiring a professional stager. They have the expertise to transform your home and create an environment that appeals to a broad range of buyers. Professional staging can be particularly beneficial for vacant properties, where furniture and décor help buyers visualize the potential of the space.

Remember, staging is about creating an emotional connection between potential buyers and your home. It allows them to see the property's full potential and imagine themselves living there. By investing in staging, you increase the chances of attracting more buyers, generating higher offers, and ultimately achieving a successful sale.

Enhancing Curb Appeal

Curb appeal is the first impression your home makes on potential buyers, so it's essential to invest time and effort in enhancing its exterior appearance. A well-maintained and visually appealing exterior creates a positive impact, captures attention, and sets the tone for the rest of the home. In this section, we will explore key considerations and strategies for enhancing curb appeal:

- Landscape maintenance: Start by ensuring that your front yard is well-maintained. Trim overgrown bushes or trees, mow the lawn, and remove any weeds or dead plants. Consider adding colorful flowers or plants to add vibrancy and freshness to the landscape. A tidy and manicured lawn creates a favorable first impression.

- Pathway and driveway: Repair any cracks or damage to the pathway and driveway. Clean and sweep these areas regularly to remove debris or leaves. If necessary, consider pressure washing or resurfacing to give them a renewed look. Enhance the pathway with attractive lighting to create an inviting atmosphere during evening showings.

- Exterior cleaning: Thoroughly clean the exterior of your home, including the walls, windows, and gutters. Power washing can be particularly effective in removing dirt, stains, and mildew from surfaces. Don't forget to clean the front door and porch area as well. A fresh and well-maintained exterior conveys a sense of pride and attention to detail.

- Paint and touch-ups: Evaluate the condition of your home's exterior paint. If the paint is peeling or faded, consider repainting to give your home a refreshed look. Pay attention to details such as window trims, shutters, and doors. Touch up any areas with chipped paint or noticeable damage to ensure a cohesive and well-maintained appearance.

- Roof and gutters: Inspect your roof for any missing or damaged shingles. Replace or repair as needed to ensure it looks well-maintained. Clean and clear your gutters to prevent any debris buildup. A sound and visually appealing roof add to the overall curb appeal of your home.

- Lighting and fixtures: Upgrade or clean your outdoor lighting fixtures to create a warm and welcoming ambiance. Consider adding landscape lighting to highlight key features or pathways. Ensure that all bulbs are in working order and provide adequate illumination during evening hours. Updated and functional fixtures add a polished touch to your home's exterior.

- Front door and porch: The front door is a focal point of your home's exterior. Consider repainting it in a bold, inviting color that complements the overall style. Add a new doormat, polish or replace the house numbers, and ensure that the doorbell and any outdoor decor are in good condition. Clean and declutter your porch area, adding tasteful furniture or accessories that create an inviting space.

- Clean windows and entryways: Clean all windows thoroughly, both inside and out, to allow maximum natural light to enter your home. Pay attention to entryways, ensuring they are free from dirt and cobwebs. Consider adding potted plants or attractive decor near the front door to add a touch of charm.

By enhancing your home's curb appeal, you create an enticing and welcoming first impression for potential buyers. The effort you invest in maintaining and beautifying the exterior sets the stage for a positive experience as buyers approach your home. Remember, a visually appealing exterior can significantly impact a buyer's perception and generate more interest in your property.

Creating Inviting Interiors

When selling your home, creating inviting interiors is key to capturing the attention and imagination of potential buyers. An inviting interior not only showcases the full potential of your home but also allows buyers to envision themselves living and thriving in the space. In this section, we will explore essential considerations and strategies for creating inviting interiors:

- Declutter and depersonalize: Start by decluttering and removing personal items that can distract buyers from envisioning themselves in the space. Clear countertops, tables, and shelves of excessive belongings. Minimize personal photographs and knick-knacks to create a clean and neutral canvas.

- Optimize furniture placement: Arrange furniture in a way that maximizes space and creates a natural flow throughout each room. Consider the focal points of each space, such as a fireplace or a scenic view, and arrange furniture to highlight these features. Avoid overcrowding and ensure that each room feels open and inviting.

- Neutral color palette: Choose a neutral color palette for your walls, furniture, and decor. Neutral tones create a sense of calm and allow potential buyers to imagine their own belongings fitting seamlessly into the space. Soft and light colors can make rooms feel more spacious and inviting.

- Lighting: Maximize natural light by opening curtains and blinds. Well-lit spaces feel more welcoming and open. Add table lamps, floor lamps, or overhead lighting as needed to ensure each room is well-illuminated. Dimmer switches can provide flexibility and create a cozy ambiance during evening showings.

- Enhance with tasteful accessories: Add tasteful accessories to complement each room's style and create a warm, inviting atmosphere. Consider incorporating throw pillows, blankets, and area rugs to add texture and comfort. Decorative items such as vases, artwork, and mirrors can also enhance the overall aesthetic and charm of the space.

- Fresh and clean: Ensure that your home is clean and fresh-smelling. Deep clean carpets, floors, and surfaces. Eliminate any odors by properly ventilating the space and using subtle air fresheners or diffusers with a neutral scent. A clean and fresh environment contributes to a positive experience for potential buyers.

- Create welcoming vignettes: Style key areas of your home with inviting vignettes that showcase its potential uses. For example, stage a cozy reading nook with a comfortable chair, side table, and a bookshelf. Create an inviting dining table setting with attractive tableware and centerpieces. These vignettes help buyers imagine the possibilities and make a strong emotional connection.

- Pay attention to details: Small details can make a significant impact on the overall impression of your interiors. Ensure that fixtures, such as doorknobs, faucets, and light switches, are clean and in good condition. Replace any worn-out or dated hardware to give a fresh and updated look.

Remember, the goal is to create a space that feels welcoming, comfortable, and inspiring to potential buyers. By incorporating these strategies, you can showcase the full potential of your home and help buyers envision themselves living in the space. A well-staged and inviting interior can leave a lasting impression and increase the likelihood of a successful sale.

Balancing Personal Touches with Broad Market Appeal

When preparing your home for sale, finding the right balance between personal touches and broad market appeal is crucial. While it's important to infuse your home with a sense of warmth and personality, it's equally essential to create a space that appeals to a wide range of potential buyers. Striking this balance allows buyers to envision themselves living in the space while appreciating the unique qualities your home has to offer. Here are some strategies to achieve this balance:

- Neutralize color schemes: Opt for neutral color palettes on walls, furniture, and accessories. Neutral colors create a versatile backdrop that can appeal to a broader audience. Soft, muted tones can create a soothing atmosphere, while whites and grays can provide a clean and contemporary look. You can add pops of color through tasteful accessories and decor that can be easily changed to suit different preferences.

- Minimize personal artifacts: While it's important to create a sense of warmth, it's best to minimize personal artifacts, such as family photos and personalized collections. These items can distract potential buyers and make it difficult for them to envision themselves in the space. Instead, showcase more generic artwork, tasteful wall decor, and other visually appealing pieces that complement the overall aesthetic.

- Style with versatility in mind: When selecting furniture and decor, aim for a style that has broad appeal. Opt for classic, timeless pieces that can accommodate various tastes and design preferences. Avoid overly trendy or niche styles that might limit the market's appeal. By choosing versatile pieces, you create a space that can easily transition to suit a buyer's personal style.

- Focus on functionality: Emphasize the functionality and versatility of each space. Arrange furniture in a way that showcases the purpose of each room, allowing potential buyers to understand how the space can be used. Highlight the flow and potential for different activities, such as a home office, a cozy reading nook, or an entertaining area. This helps buyers see the practicality of the space beyond personal preferences.

- Showcase key features: Highlight the unique features of your home that set it apart from others on the market. This could be architectural details, custom upgrades, or desirable amenities. Showcase these features without overwhelming buyers with personal preferences. Use tasteful staging and decor to draw attention to these elements, helping potential buyers envision the added value they bring.

- Seek feedback and advice: Consult with your real estate agent or staging professional for guidance on striking the right balance between personal touches and broad market appeal. They can offer insights based on their experience in the local market and provide recommendations on how to present your home in a way that appeals to a wide range of buyers.

Remember, the goal is to create a welcoming and inviting space that allows potential buyers to see themselves living in your home. By striking the right balance between personal touches and broad market appeal, you increase the likelihood of attracting more interested buyers and achieving a successful sale.

PRICING STRATEGIES: DETERMINING THE RIGHT LISTING PRICE

Pricing your home correctly is a critical factor in the success of your home sale. Setting the right listing price can attract potential buyers, generate interest, and ultimately lead to a successful sale. However, determining the optimal listing price is not a simple task. It requires careful consideration of various factors, market conditions, and effective pricing strategies. In this chapter, we will delve into the art of pricing strategies and explore the key considerations for determining the right listing price for your home.

To start, we will explore the importance of conducting a comparative market analysis (CMA). A CMA involves evaluating recently sold properties that are similar to yours in terms of location, size, features, and condition. Analyzing the sold prices of these comparable properties provides valuable insights into the market trends and serves as a benchmark for pricing your home. By conducting a thorough CMA, you can gain a better understanding of the value of your home in relation to recent market activity.

Next, we will discuss the significance of seeking professional guidance from a trusted real estate agent. An experienced agent has access to comprehensive market data, a deep understanding of local market conditions, and the expertise to interpret and apply that information to determine an appropriate listing price for your home. Their insights and guidance can help you navigate the complexities of pricing, ensuring that your home is positioned competitively in the market.

Furthermore, we will consider the impact of market conditions on pricing strategies. The current state of the real estate market, whether it's a seller's market or a buyer's market, can influence your pricing approach. Understanding the supply and demand dynamics, competition levels, and buyer preferences in your local market is essential for determining the right listing price that aligns with market conditions.

Throughout this chapter, we will also explore additional pricing strategies and factors to consider. These may include the unique features and upgrades of your home, the condition of the property, the location, and any recent market trends or economic factors that may impact pricing decisions. We will discuss the importance of balancing market realities with your goals and expectations to arrive at a pricing strategy that maximizes your chances of achieving a successful sale.

Remember, pricing your home correctly is a delicate balance that requires a combination of market knowledge, data analysis, and strategic thinking. By understanding the principles of pricing strategies and considering the unique attributes of your home and the market, you can confidently determine the right listing price and set the stage for a successful home sale.

Comparative Market Analysis (CMA)

A Comparative Market Analysis (CMA) is a crucial tool used in real estate to determine the value of a property by analyzing recent sales data of comparable properties in the same area. It provides valuable insights into the current market conditions, trends, and a benchmark for pricing a home. Here are key aspects of a CMA:

- Evaluating Comparable Properties: The first step in conducting a CMA is identifying properties that are similar to the subject property in terms of location, size, features, and condition. These comparable properties, or "comps," should have recently sold in the same neighborhood or nearby area.

- Analyzing Sold Prices: Once the comparable properties have been identified, the next step is to analyze their sold prices. This involves examining the actual sale prices, as well as other relevant information such as the number of days on the market, any price reductions, and the terms of the sale.

- Adjusting for Differences: While comparing sold prices, it's important to account for any differences between the subject property and the comparables. Factors such as square footage, number of bedrooms and bathrooms, upgrades, and overall condition can significantly impact the value. Adjustments are made to the sold prices of the comparable properties to account for these differences, providing a more accurate estimate of the subject property's value.

- Assessing Market Trends: A CMA also helps identify market trends and patterns. By analyzing multiple comparable properties, trends in pricing, market activity, and buyer preferences can be identified. This information provides insights into the current state of the market and helps determine an appropriate listing price.

- Informing Pricing Decisions: The information gathered from a CMA serves as a guide for determining the right listing price for a property. It helps sellers understand the potential market value of their home and ensures that the listing price is competitive, attracting potential buyers while still maximizing the return on investment.

Real estate agents often use their expertise and local market knowledge to perform a comprehensive CMA for their clients. They interpret the data, make adjustments, and provide insights on pricing strategies based on the findings. By utilizing a CMA, sellers can make informed decisions, set realistic pricing expectations, and increase their chances of a successful sale in the dynamic real estate market.

Seeking Professional Guidance From A Trusted Real Estate Agent

When selling your home, seeking professional guidance from a trusted real estate agent is a smart decision that can greatly impact the success of your sale. An experienced agent brings valuable expertise, market knowledge, and resources to the table, helping you navigate the complexities of the real estate process with confidence. Here are key reasons why seeking professional guidance from a trusted real estate agent is essential:

- Local Market Expertise: Real estate agents have a deep understanding of the local market dynamics, including current trends, pricing patterns, and buyer preferences. They stay up-to-date with the latest market data and can provide valuable insights into pricing strategies, timing, and marketing techniques specific to your area. Their knowledge helps you make informed decisions and position your home competitively in the market.

- Pricing Accuracy: Determining the right listing price for your home is crucial, and it requires a comprehensive analysis of market data and comparable properties. Real estate agents have access to professional tools and resources that enable them to perform accurate pricing analyses. They can assess the unique features of your home, consider market conditions, and provide a realistic pricing strategy that balances your goals and market expectations.

- Marketing and Exposure: Real estate agents excel in marketing homes effectively to attract potential buyers. They have a wide network of contacts, access to multiple listing services (MLS), and various marketing channels to promote your property to a broad audience. They know how to highlight the unique selling points of your home, create compelling listing descriptions, and leverage professional photography and virtual tours to maximize exposure.

- Negotiation Skills: Negotiating with potential buyers is a critical aspect of the home selling process. Real estate agents have honed their negotiation skills through years of experience. They advocate for your interests, navigate through offers and counteroffers, and strive to secure the best possible terms and price for your home. Their expertise can help you navigate complex negotiations and achieve a favorable outcome.

- Transaction Management: Selling a home involves a multitude of paperwork, deadlines, and legalities. A trusted real estate agent will guide you through the entire transaction process, ensuring that all necessary documents are properly completed and submitted. They coordinate inspections, appraisals, and other necessary steps, providing peace of mind and ensuring a smooth and timely transaction.

- Professional Network: Real estate agents have a network of professionals they work with, including inspectors, appraisers, mortgage brokers, and attorneys. They can recommend reliable and reputable professionals to assist you throughout the selling process, saving you time and effort in finding trustworthy service providers.

By seeking professional guidance from a trusted real estate agent, you tap into their expertise, market knowledge, and network, empowering you to make informed decisions and navigate the selling process with confidence. Their guidance can increase your chances of a successful sale, save you time and stress, and ensure that you achieve your selling goals.

The Impact of Market Conditions On Pricing Strategies

Market conditions play a significant role in determining the most effective pricing strategies when selling your home. The state of the real estate market at the time of listing can influence buyer behavior, competition levels, and overall demand for properties. To maximize your chances of a successful sale, it's essential to understand how market conditions can impact pricing strategies. Here are key considerations:

- Seller's Market: In a seller's market, there is high demand for properties and limited inventory. Buyers often compete for available homes, which can drive up prices. In this scenario, a strategic pricing strategy may involve setting a listing price at the higher end of the market range to capitalize on buyer enthusiasm and potential bidding wars. However, it's crucial to ensure the price remains within a reasonable range to avoid deterring buyers or appraisal issues.

- Buyer's Market: In a buyer's market, there is an abundance of available properties and fewer buyers. This can create a more competitive environment for sellers. In such conditions, a pricing strategy may involve setting a listing price at the lower end of the market range to attract buyers and stand out among the competition. This approach aims to generate more interest and potentially prompt multiple offers.

- Balanced Market: In a balanced market, the supply of homes for sale matches the demand from buyers. Prices tend to be stable, and there is a healthy balance between sellers and buyers. Pricing strategies in a balanced market often involve setting a listing price that aligns closely with recent comparable sales and market trends. It's important to remain competitive while also considering the unique features and selling points of your property.

- Seasonal Fluctuations: Market conditions can also be influenced by seasonal fluctuations. For example, spring and summer tend to be busier seasons in real estate, with increased buyer activity. In these seasons, pricing strategies may involve setting a listing price that reflects the heightened demand and buyer enthusiasm. However, it's essential to assess local market dynamics and consult with a real estate agent to determine the optimal pricing approach for your specific area and time of year.

- Economic Factors: Economic factors, such as interest rates, employment rates, and consumer confidence, can impact market conditions and buyer behavior. A strong economy can drive increased demand and potentially support higher prices. Conversely, economic downturns may lead to reduced buyer activity and a need for more conservative pricing strategies.

When determining pricing strategies, it's crucial to consult with a trusted real estate agent who has a deep understanding of the local market. They can analyze market conditions, assess buyer demand, and provide insights on the most effective pricing approach for your specific situation. Their expertise and knowledge of market dynamics will help you position your home competitively, attract potential buyers, and maximize your chances of a successful sale in any market condition.

MARKETING YOUR PROPERTY: EFFECTIVE STRATEGIES FOR MAXIMUM EXPOSURE

Marketing your property is a crucial step in the home-selling process. To attract potential buyers and achieve a successful sale, it's essential to implement effective marketing strategies that generate maximum exposure for your property. In this chapter, we will explore a range of proven marketing techniques and strategies that will help you showcase your property's unique features, attract qualified buyers, and stand out in the competitive real estate market.

The world of real estate marketing has evolved significantly in recent years, with advancements in technology and an increased emphasis on digital platforms. We will delve into the power of online marketing, including the utilization of professional photography, virtual tours, and compelling listing descriptions that highlight the best aspects of your property. We will explore how to optimize your online presence through various listing platforms, social media channels, and targeted online advertising to reach a wider audience and generate more interest.

In addition to digital marketing, we will discuss the importance of traditional marketing methods that continue to be effective. We will explore strategies such as print advertising, open houses, and direct mail campaigns to engage with potential buyers and create a lasting impression. We will also discuss the significance of signage, both on the property itself and in the surrounding area, to capture the attention of passersby and generate local interest.

Furthermore, we will delve into the importance of staging and presentation in the marketing process. We will explore how to create visually appealing interiors and enhance curb appeal to make a strong first impression on potential buyers. We will also discuss the value of professional staging services and how they can elevate the presentation of your property.

Additionally, we will address the importance of accurately targeting your marketing efforts to reach the most qualified buyers. We will explore strategies for identifying and reaching out to potential buyer demographics, such as first-time homebuyers, downsizers, or investors, ensuring that your marketing efforts are focused and effective.

Throughout this chapter, we will emphasize the significance of collaborating with a trusted real estate agent who has expertise in marketing properties. They can provide guidance, create a comprehensive marketing plan, and leverage their network and resources to maximize exposure for your property.

By implementing effective marketing strategies, you can increase the visibility of your property, attract more qualified buyers, and enhance your chances of achieving a successful sale. Let's explore the world of real estate marketing and equip you with the tools and knowledge to effectively market your property for maximum exposure.

Online Marketing

In today's digital age, online marketing has become a powerful tool for promoting and showcasing properties to a wide audience of potential buyers. Leveraging various online platforms and strategies is essential to maximize exposure and generate interest in your property. In this section, we will explore key components of effective online marketing for your home:

- Professional Photography: High-quality, professionally captured photographs are crucial for making a strong first impression online. Invest in professional photography services to showcase your property in the best possible light. Quality images help potential buyers visualize the space and generate initial interest.

- Compelling Listing Descriptions: Craft engaging and informative listing descriptions that highlight the key features and selling points of your home. Use descriptive language to paint a vivid picture and entice potential buyers. Focus on unique attributes, such as updated amenities, architectural details, or the property's proximity to amenities and attractions.

- Virtual Tours and Video Walkthroughs: Enhance your online marketing efforts by incorporating virtual tours or video walkthroughs. These interactive experiences allow potential buyers to virtually explore your property from the comfort of their own homes. They provide a more immersive and realistic view of the space, generating higher levels of engagement and interest.

- Online Listing Platforms: Utilize popular online listing platforms, such as real estate websites and portals, to showcase your property. These platforms attract a large audience of potential buyers actively searching for homes. Optimize your listings by providing accurate and detailed information, including property specifications, pricing, and contact details.

- Social Media Marketing: Leverage the power of social media platforms to reach a broader audience and engage with potential buyers. Create professional profiles for your property on platforms like Facebook, Instagram, and Twitter. Regularly post visually appealing photos, virtual tours, and engaging content related to your property. Use relevant hashtags and engage with online communities to expand your reach.

- Targeted Online Advertising: Consider utilizing targeted online advertising to reach specific buyer demographics or geographic areas. Platforms like Google Ads and social media advertising allow you to define your target audience and display your property listing to those most likely to be interested. This ensures that your marketing efforts are focused and cost-effective.

- Website and Landing Pages: If you have a dedicated property website or landing page, optimize it to attract and engage potential buyers. Ensure that the site is visually appealing, easy to navigate, and provides comprehensive information about your property. Include high-quality images, virtual tours, and contact forms to capture leads and facilitate direct communication with interested buyers.

Remember to regularly monitor and update your online marketing efforts to stay current and relevant. Analyze data and feedback to refine your strategies and make necessary adjustments. By leveraging the power of online marketing, you can effectively showcase your property to a wide audience, generate interest, and increase your chances of a successful sale.

Traditional Marketing

While online marketing has become increasingly prominent, traditional marketing methods still hold value when it comes to promoting your property. These strategies can complement your online efforts and help you reach a broader audience, including those who may not be as active online. In this section, we will explore key components of traditional marketing for your property:

- Print Advertising: Utilize print media, such as newspapers, magazines, and local real estate publications, to advertise your property. Place eye-catching ads that include high-quality photos, key details, and contact information. Target publications that have a readership that aligns with your target buyer demographics.

- Yard Signs and Flyers: Place a prominent "For Sale" sign in your front yard, including your agent's contact information. Yard signs attract the attention of passersby and generate local interest. Additionally, create professional flyers or brochures that provide an overview of your property's features and distribute them at open houses, local businesses, and community bulletin boards.

- Open Houses: Hosting open houses provides an opportunity for potential buyers to view your property in person and get a feel for its layout and features. Advertise open houses through various channels, including online platforms, local print media, and signage in the neighborhood. Consider offering refreshments or special incentives to attract more visitors.

- Direct Mail Campaigns: Send targeted direct mail campaigns to potential buyers in your area. This could include postcards, flyers, or personalized letters introducing your property. Target specific neighborhoods or demographics that align with your ideal buyer profile to maximize the impact of your direct mail efforts.

- Networking and Referrals: Leverage your personal and professional networks to spread the word about your property. Inform friends, family, neighbors, and colleagues that your home is on the market. They may know someone who is looking to buy or can help refer potential buyers to you.

- Local Community Engagement: Get involved in your local community and establish your property's presence. Sponsor local events or sports teams, participate in neighborhood associations, or support charitable initiatives. This involvement can create positive associations with your property and attract potential buyers who appreciate community engagement.

- Real Estate Agent's Network: Rely on the network of your trusted real estate agent. They have connections within the industry and can tap into their network of other agents who may have interested buyers. Collaborate with your agent to ensure your property is promoted through their network, increasing exposure to qualified buyers.

Remember to tailor your traditional marketing efforts to suit your target audience and local market conditions. The goal is to create awareness and generate interest in your property through various offline channels. By combining traditional marketing with online strategies, you can reach a wider range of potential buyers and maximize your property's exposure, increasing your chances of finding the right buyer and achieving a successful sale.

WORKING WITH REAL ESTATE AGENTS: FINDING THE RIGHT PROFESSIONAL

When selling your home, partnering with a skilled and reliable real estate agent can make a significant difference in the success of your sale. A knowledgeable agent can provide valuable guidance, market expertise, and negotiation skills to help you navigate the complex real estate process. In this section, we will explore key considerations for finding the right real estate professional to assist you:

- Research and Referrals: Start by conducting thorough research and gathering recommendations from trusted sources. Seek referrals from friends, family, or colleagues who have recently sold their homes. Take advantage of online platforms, such as real estate websites or local directories, to read reviews and gather information about different agents in your area.

- Experience and Expertise: Look for an agent who has substantial experience and a proven track record in the local market. Consider their knowledge of the neighborhood, their success in selling properties similar to yours, and their familiarity with current market trends. An experienced agent can provide valuable insights, pricing strategies, and effective marketing techniques.

- Communication and Compatibility: Effective communication is crucial when working with a real estate agent. Look for an agent who is attentive, responsive, and demonstrates clear and open communication. They should listen to your needs, understand your goals, and keep you informed throughout the selling process. Compatibility and a good rapport with your agent are also important for a smooth and successful working relationship.

- Local Market Knowledge: A real estate agent with in-depth knowledge of the local market is a valuable asset. They should be aware of recent sales activity, pricing trends, and neighborhood dynamics. Their understanding of the local market can help you set an appropriate listing price, identify potential buyers, and position your property competitively.

- Marketing Strategies: Evaluate the marketing strategies and resources that the agent utilizes to promote properties. Inquire about their online marketing efforts, professional photography, virtual tours, and presence on relevant listing platforms. A proactive agent with a strong marketing plan will maximize the exposure of your property and attract a wider range of potential buyers.

- Professional Network: Consider an agent's network of connections within the industry. A well-connected agent can tap into their network of other professionals, such as inspectors, appraisers, mortgage brokers, and attorneys, who may be instrumental in the selling process. A solid professional network ensures that you have access to reliable and trustworthy resources.

- Commission and Fees: Discuss the agent's commission structure and any associated fees upfront. Understand the terms of the agreement, including the length of the listing contract and any exclusivity clauses. While the commission is an important consideration, it should not be the sole determining factor in choosing an agent. Focus on finding a qualified professional who offers the best value for their services.

- Trust your Instincts: Trust your instincts when evaluating potential agents. Pay attention to how comfortable you feel during your initial meetings and whether the agent instills confidence and trust. Choose someone who is genuinely interested in your goals, understands your priorities, and has a genuine commitment to achieving a successful sale.

By considering these key factors and conducting thorough research, you can find the right real estate professional to guide you through the home selling process. A skilled agent with a strong understanding of the local market, effective communication skills, and a proactive approach will help you navigate the complexities of selling your home and increase your chances of a successful and smooth transaction.

THE ART OF NEGOTIATION: GETTING THE BEST DEAL

Negotiation is a critical aspect of the home selling process, and mastering the art of negotiation can significantly impact the outcome of your sale. Effective negotiation skills can help you secure the best deal, maximize your profits, and navigate through potential obstacles. In this chapter, we will delve into the strategies, techniques, and mindset required to excel in negotiation and achieve optimal results.

Negotiation in real estate is a dynamic and multifaceted process that involves interactions with potential buyers, their agents, and other stakeholders. It requires a balance of assertiveness, empathy, and strategic thinking. Whether it's negotiating the sale price, contract terms, or contingencies, having a solid grasp of negotiation principles is essential.

We will explore key considerations for successful negotiation, starting with thorough preparation. Understanding your goals, knowing your property's value, and being aware of market conditions are crucial in setting realistic expectations and positioning yourself for a successful negotiation.

Building rapport and effective communication skills are essential for establishing a positive and productive negotiation environment. We will discuss active listening, clear communication, and the importance of understanding the motivations and interests of the other party. By fostering open and respectful dialogue, you can find common ground and explore mutually beneficial solutions.

Negotiation involves give-and-take, and we will explore strategies for making concessions strategically. Knowing when to stand firm and when to be flexible can greatly influence the outcome. We will discuss various negotiation techniques, such as creating win-win scenarios, finding creative solutions, and utilizing leverage points to your advantage.

Additionally, we will address the role of emotions in negotiation and the importance of maintaining a composed and rational mindset. Understanding and managing emotions, both your own and those of the other party, can help navigate through potential conflicts and maintain a constructive negotiation process.

Throughout this chapter, we will emphasize the significance of working with a skilled real estate agent who is experienced in negotiation. They can offer valuable guidance, act as a buffer between you and the other party, and advocate for your interests. Collaborating with an agent who possesses strong negotiation skills will give you a competitive edge and increase your chances of achieving the best possible deal.

Mastering the art of negotiation is a valuable skill that can benefit you in various aspects of life, not just in real estate. By understanding negotiation principles, preparing thoroughly, and adopting effective strategies, you can confidently navigate the negotiation process and secure a favorable outcome. Let's explore the art of negotiation and equip you with the tools and knowledge to get the best deal when selling your home.

Key Considerations for Successful Negotiation

Successful negotiation requires careful planning, effective communication, and a strategic approach. Whether you're negotiating the sale price, contract terms, or contingencies, keeping these key considerations in mind can significantly enhance your chances of achieving a favorable outcome. Here are some important factors to consider when entering into negotiations:

- Preparation: Thorough preparation is crucial before entering into negotiations. Understand your goals, priorities, and the limits of your negotiation range. Research market trends, recent sales data, and comparable properties to have a realistic understanding of the property's value. Prepare counterarguments and anticipate potential objections or concerns from the other party.

- Active Listening and Understanding: Effective communication starts with active listening and seeking to understand the motivations and interests of the other party. Pay attention to their words, tone, and body language to gain insight into their needs and preferences. By understanding their perspective, you can tailor your approach and propose solutions that address their concerns while meeting your own objectives.

- Building Rapport: Building rapport and establishing a positive relationship with the other party can enhance the negotiation process. Find common ground, be respectful, and demonstrate empathy. By creating a cooperative and collaborative atmosphere, you increase the likelihood of finding mutually beneficial solutions.

- Flexibility and Creativity: Negotiation often involves finding compromises and creative solutions. Be open to exploring different options and consider alternatives that may meet both parties' interests. Flexibility in your negotiation approach can lead to win-win outcomes and a smoother negotiation process.

- Patience and Emotional Control: Negotiations can be intense and emotional, but it's important to remain patient and maintain emotional control. Avoid making impulsive decisions or reacting impulsively to counteroffers or disagreements. Stay focused on your goals and maintain a calm and composed demeanor throughout the negotiation process.

- Utilizing Leverage: Identify and utilize any leverage points you may have during the negotiation. Leverage can come from factors such as market conditions, property desirability, or unique circumstances. Highlighting these advantages can strengthen your negotiating position and increase your bargaining power.

- Seek Professional Guidance: Consider working with a skilled real estate agent who has expertise in negotiation. They can provide valuable guidance, offer objective advice, and act as a buffer between you and the other party. An experienced agent can bring a wealth of knowledge, negotiation strategies, and market insights to help you secure the best possible deal.

- Win-Win Solutions: Aim for win-win outcomes where both parties feel satisfied with the negotiation results. While it's natural to focus on your own interests, considering the other party's needs can lead to more successful and long-lasting agreements. Look for creative solutions that address both parties' objectives and build a foundation for future cooperation.

By keeping these key considerations in mind, you can approach negotiations with confidence and increase your chances of achieving a successful outcome. Effective preparation, active listening, flexibility, and maintaining emotional control are crucial elements for navigating negotiations and securing a favorable deal when selling your home.

Building Rapport and Effective Communication Skills

Building rapport and effective communication skills are vital components of successful negotiations. Establishing a positive connection with the other party fosters trust, understanding, and a cooperative environment. Effective communication allows for clear and open dialogue, ensuring that both parties' interests and perspectives are heard and considered. Here are key points to consider when it comes to building rapport and honing your communication skills:

- Active Listening: Active listening is a fundamental aspect of effective communication. It involves giving your full attention to the other party, seeking to understand their viewpoint, and responding appropriately. Avoid interrupting and genuinely listen to their words, tone, and non-verbal cues. By actively listening, you demonstrate respect and empathy, which can lead to a more productive negotiation process.

- Empathy and Understanding: Putting yourself in the shoes of the other party is crucial for building rapport and establishing a positive connection. Show empathy by acknowledging their perspective and understanding their needs and concerns. This helps create a collaborative atmosphere and allows for a more productive exchange of ideas.

- Clarity and Conciseness: Communicate your thoughts and ideas clearly and concisely. Use simple and straightforward language to avoid misunderstandings. Organize your thoughts before speaking and be prepared to articulate your points effectively. Clarity in your communication helps build credibility and ensures that your message is understood.

- Non-Verbal Communication: Pay attention to non-verbal communication, as it can convey messages just as strongly as words. Maintain eye contact, use appropriate facial expressions, and be aware of your body language. By being conscious of your non-verbal cues and being attuned to the other party's signals, you can foster a sense of trust and openness.

- Respectful and Constructive Dialogue: Maintain a respectful and constructive dialogue throughout the negotiation process. Avoid personal attacks or defensive behaviors. Instead, focus on the issues at hand and present your arguments or counteroffers in a professional and courteous manner. Respecting the other party's opinions, even if you disagree, helps maintain a positive rapport and fosters collaboration.

- Finding Common Ground: Look for common ground and shared interests with the other party. Identify areas where you both agree and build upon those points to find mutually beneficial solutions. Establishing shared goals or objectives can bridge differences and create a foundation for compromise.

- Adaptability and Flexibility: Effective communication requires adaptability and flexibility. Adjust your communication style to accommodate the preferences and communication style of the other party. Be open to different approaches and be willing to modify your strategy if necessary. Adapting to the needs of the negotiation process can help build rapport and facilitate effective communication.

Building rapport and honing your communication skills are ongoing processes that require practice and conscious effort. By actively listening, showing empathy, maintaining clarity, and fostering respectful dialogue, you can establish a positive rapport and enhance your ability to communicate effectively during negotiations. These skills lay the foundation for a successful negotiation process and increase the likelihood of achieving mutually beneficial outcomes when selling your home.

The Role of Emotions in Negotiation

Emotions play a significant role in the negotiation process, influencing the attitudes, behaviors, and decisions of all parties involved. Recognizing and managing emotions effectively can greatly impact the outcome of a negotiation. Here are key points to consider regarding the role of emotions in negotiation:

- Emotional Awareness: Understanding your own emotions and being aware of the emotions of the other party is crucial. Recognize the emotions that arise during the negotiation process, such as excitement, frustration, or anxiety. Pay attention to non-verbal cues and verbal expressions that indicate the other party's emotional state. By being emotionally aware, you can respond more effectively and navigate the negotiation process with greater insight.

- Emotional Control: Emotional control is essential for maintaining a rational and objective mindset during negotiations. Emotions, if not managed properly, can lead to impulsive decision-making, aggressive behavior, or an inability to find common ground. Stay composed, manage stress, and make decisions based on sound judgment rather than reacting purely on emotions. Emphasize the importance of maintaining a calm and respectful demeanor throughout the negotiation process.

- Empathy and Understanding: Emotions can shape perceptions and influence decision-making. Developing empathy and understanding towards the other party's emotions can foster a more constructive negotiation environment. Put yourself in their shoes, acknowledge their concerns, and show empathy towards their perspective. By understanding their emotions, you can tailor your approach and propose solutions that address their underlying needs.

- Emotional Triggers and Biases: Recognize that certain issues or triggers may elicit strong emotional responses from either party. Be aware of your own emotional triggers and biases that may cloud judgment or impede compromise. Seek to address these triggers and biases by focusing on the objective facts, remaining open to different perspectives, and reframing the situation to promote a more collaborative approach.

- Building Trust: Emotions play a crucial role in building trust between the negotiating parties. Trust is essential for effective communication, information sharing, and collaboration. By demonstrating emotional intelligence, empathy, and maintaining a trustworthy demeanor, you can foster an environment of trust and goodwill. Building trust encourages open and honest communication, making it easier to find mutually beneficial outcomes.

- Emotional Appeals: In some instances, emotions can be intentionally used as a persuasive tool in negotiations. Emotional appeals can be effective in influencing the other party's decision-making process. However, it is important to use emotional appeals ethically and with caution, ensuring that they align with the facts and do not manipulate or exploit the other party's emotions.

- Focus on Interests: Emotions can sometimes cloud judgment and steer negotiations towards positional bargaining rather than focusing on underlying interests. By recognizing the emotions at play and refocusing the discussion on shared interests, you can steer the negotiation towards a more collaborative and constructive path. Identifying and addressing underlying interests helps to uncover potential solutions that satisfy both parties' needs.

Understanding and managing emotions during negotiations is a skill that can be developed over time. By cultivating emotional awareness, maintaining emotional control, showing empathy, and focusing on trust and shared interests, you can navigate the negotiation process more effectively. Emotions, when managed properly, can be channeled towards positive outcomes, leading to more successful and mutually satisfying agreements when selling your home.

LEGAL CONSIDERATIONS AND DISCLOSURES

When selling your home, it is essential to understand and comply with various legal considerations and disclosures. These legal obligations help protect both the buyer and seller and ensure transparency throughout the transaction. Failure to fulfill these requirements can lead to legal complications and potential financial liabilities. In this section, we will explore key legal considerations and disclosures when selling your home:

- Property Disclosures: Most jurisdictions require sellers to provide certain disclosures about the property's condition and any known issues. These disclosures typically cover aspects such as structural defects, past repairs, water damage, pest infestations, and environmental hazards. It is crucial to disclose any material facts that could affect the buyer's decision-making process. Consult with your real estate agent or attorney to ensure you meet the disclosure requirements specific to your location.

- Lead-Based Paint Disclosure: If your home was built before 1978, federal law in the United States requires you to provide a lead-based paint disclosure. This disclosure informs buyers about the potential presence of lead-based paint and any known hazards. Sellers must provide an informational pamphlet and include specific language in the sales contract regarding lead-based paint.

- Homeowner's Association (HOA) Disclosures: If your property is part of a homeowner's association, you may need to provide HOA disclosures to the buyer. These disclosures include information about HOA rules, fees, assessments, and any pending litigation or violations. Buyers have the right to review these disclosures and understand their rights and obligations as members of the HOA.

- Local and State Regulations: Familiarize yourself with local and state regulations regarding real estate transactions. These may include specific disclosure requirements, zoning restrictions, or environmental regulations that impact the sale of your property. Consult with a local real estate professional or attorney to ensure compliance with these regulations.

- Contractual Obligations: When entering into a purchase agreement with the buyer, it is crucial to understand and fulfill your contractual obligations. This includes adhering to agreed-upon timelines, providing necessary documentation, and meeting any contingencies outlined in the contract. Failure to fulfill these obligations can lead to legal disputes and potential financial consequences.

- Title and Ownership: Ensuring clear title and ownership of the property is essential. Buyers typically request a title search to identify any existing liens, encumbrances, or ownership disputes. As the seller, you are responsible for providing a marketable title, free of any undisclosed issues. Consider obtaining title insurance to protect against any unforeseen title-related claims or disputes.

- Legal Representation: It is advisable to seek legal representation from a real estate attorney experienced in property transactions. They can review contracts, assist with disclosures, and provide guidance on legal requirements specific to your situation. Having legal counsel ensures that you are well-informed and protected throughout the selling process.

- Consultation with Professionals: When in doubt about any legal considerations or disclosures, consult with professionals such as real estate agents, attorneys, or home inspectors. Their expertise can help you navigate the complexities of legal requirements and ensure compliance with all necessary obligations.

By understanding and fulfilling your legal obligations and disclosures, you protect yourself, the buyer, and the integrity of the transaction. Proper compliance with legal considerations provides transparency and peace of mind, leading to a smoother and more successful sale of your home.

UNDERSTANDING BUYER FINANCING OPTIONS

When selling your home, it is crucial to have a solid understanding of the various financing options available to potential buyers. Each buyer's financial situation is unique, and their choice of financing can impact the sale process and ultimately determine their ability to purchase your property. By familiarizing yourself with these financing options, you can effectively navigate buyer inquiries, assess their qualifications, and increase the likelihood of a successful sale. Let's explore some common buyer financing options:

- Conventional Mortgage Loans: Conventional mortgage loans are one of the most prevalent financing options for homebuyers. These loans are typically offered by banks, credit unions, and mortgage lenders. Conventional loans require a down payment, which can vary but is often around 20% of the purchase price. Lenders assess the buyer's creditworthiness, income stability, and debt-to-income ratio to determine loan eligibility and interest rates. Conventional loans offer flexibility in terms of loan duration and interest rate options.

- Federal Housing Administration (FHA) Loans: FHA loans are backed by the Federal Housing Administration, making them accessible to buyers who may not qualify for conventional loans due to lower credit scores or a limited down payment. FHA loans require a lower down payment (often as low as 3.5% of the purchase price) and have more lenient qualification criteria. However, borrowers are required to pay mortgage insurance premiums. Sellers should be aware of certain property condition requirements for FHA loans, as they may impact the eligibility of the property.

- Department of Veterans Affairs (VA) Loans: VA loans are available to eligible military veterans, active-duty service members, and surviving spouses. These loans are guaranteed by the Department of Veterans Affairs and offer favorable terms, including no down payment requirements and competitive interest rates. Sellers should be aware of specific VA loan appraisal and inspection requirements, as they may affect the sale process.

- United States Department of Agriculture (USDA) Loans: USDA loans are designed to assist buyers in rural and suburban areas. They are offered by the United States Department of Agriculture and provide low to moderate-income borrowers with attractive loan terms, including no down payment requirements. Eligibility for USDA loans is based on income limits and property location. Sellers should be aware of specific USDA loan requirements and property eligibility criteria when considering offers from buyers using this financing option.

- Jumbo Loans: Jumbo loans are used for high-priced properties that exceed the conventional loan limits set by government-sponsored enterprises like Fannie Mae and Freddie Mac. These loans have higher borrowing limits, but they also typically require larger down payments and stricter qualification criteria. Buyers seeking jumbo loans often have strong credit histories and higher income levels.

- Cash Buyers: Cash buyers do not require financing and pay for the property entirely with cash. Cash offers can be appealing to sellers as they eliminate the need for the buyer to secure financing and can expedite the closing process. Cash buyers may include investors, individuals who have sold a previous property, or those who have accumulated savings. Sellers should still evaluate cash buyers based on their ability to provide proof of funds and ensure they are qualified to complete the transaction.

Understanding these buyer financing options allows you to assess potential buyers effectively and evaluate the strength of their offers. It's important to keep in mind that each financing option has its own requirements and considerations that may impact the transaction timeline and specific terms. Working with a knowledgeable real estate agent can help you navigate the complexities of buyer financing and ensure that you choose the most qualified buyer for your property.

When considering offers, sellers should carefully review pre-approval or prequalification letters from lenders to verify the buyer's financial capability. It's advisable to consult with your own real estate attorney or financial advisor to fully understand the implications of each financing option and its impact on the sale process

HANDLING MULTIPLE OFFERS: STRATEGIES FOR EVALUATING AND CHOOSING THE BEST

Receiving multiple offers on your property can be an exciting but challenging situation to navigate. It presents an opportunity to maximize your sale price and choose the most qualified buyer. However, evaluating and choosing the best offer requires careful consideration and strategic decision-making. In this section, we will explore effective strategies for evaluating multiple offers and selecting the one that best aligns with your goals:

- Review Offer Terms: Start by thoroughly reviewing each offer and understanding its terms. Consider factors such as the offered purchase price, financing contingencies, down payment amount, requested closing date, and any additional contingencies or special conditions. Look for offers that align with your preferences and have terms that meet your specific needs.

- Evaluate Buyer Qualifications: Assess the qualifications of each buyer to determine their ability to proceed with the transaction. Review their financing options, down payment amount, creditworthiness, and any pre-approval or prequalification letters provided. Consider the buyer's level of commitment, financial stability, and likelihood of successfully closing the deal.

- Consider Contingencies: Pay close attention to contingencies included in each offer. Common contingencies include home inspection, appraisal, and financing contingencies. Evaluate the feasibility and potential impact of these contingencies on the sale process. Offers with fewer or more favorable contingencies may be more attractive, depending on your specific circumstances and the condition of your property.

- Analyze Buyer's Motivation: Understanding the motivations of each buyer can provide valuable insight into their commitment and willingness to negotiate. Consider factors such as their timeline, reasons for buying, and level of interest in your property. Buyers who demonstrate a genuine interest and strong motivation may be more likely to work through any challenges and proceed with the transaction smoothly.

- Assess Financing Options: Evaluate the financing options presented by each buyer. Consider the type of loan they are using, the lender's reputation, and the stability of their financing arrangement. Buyers with solid financing options, such as pre-approved conventional loans or cash offers, may offer more certainty and a smoother transaction process.

- Evaluate Contingent Offers: If any of the offers are contingent upon the sale of the buyer's current home, carefully evaluate the feasibility and timeline of their contingency. Assess the market conditions and demand for their property, as well as the buyer's pricing strategy and marketing efforts. Contingent offers may introduce additional risks and uncertainties, so weigh these factors against the potential benefits.

- Consult with Your Real Estate Agent: Seek guidance from your real estate agent throughout the evaluation process. They can provide valuable insights and help you assess the strengths and weaknesses of each offer. Leverage their expertise and market knowledge to make an informed decision.

- Counteroffer or Request Best and Final: If none of the initial offers meet your expectations, you can consider countering or requesting a "best and final" offer from the interested parties. This allows you to provide feedback or adjust the terms to better align with your goals. However, be mindful that this approach may lead to some buyers withdrawing their offers, so carefully assess the potential risks and benefits.

- Trust Your Instincts: Ultimately, trust your instincts and prioritize your own goals and preferences. While financial considerations are important, factors such as the buyer's responsiveness, professionalism, and overall fit with your vision for the sale may also influence your decision. Consider the overall package each offer presents, including the combination of price, terms, and buyer qualifications.

Handling multiple offers requires thoughtful analysis and consideration of various factors. By carefully evaluating each offer's terms, buyer qualifications, contingencies, financing options, and motivations, you can make an informed decision that best aligns with your goals and maximizes the value of your property.

CLOSING THE DEAL: THE SALES CONTRACT AND ESCROW PROCESS

Closing the deal on the sale of your home involves executing a sales contract and navigating the escrow process. This final stage of the transaction requires attention to detail, adherence to legal requirements, and coordination between all parties involved. In this section, we will explore the key components of the sales contract and the escrow process:

- Sales Contract: The sales contract is a legally binding agreement between the buyer and seller that outlines the terms and conditions of the sale. It includes details such as the purchase price, closing date, financing terms, contingencies, and any specific agreements reached between the parties. The contract may also include provisions related to property inspections, repairs, and disclosures. It is essential to review the contract carefully and ensure that all terms are accurately reflected before signing.

- Escrow Officer and Escrow Process: Once the sales contract is executed, the transaction typically enters the escrow process. An escrow officer, who acts as a neutral third party, is responsible for managing the escrow process. They ensure that all terms and conditions of the contract are met, handle the transfer of funds, and facilitate the exchange of legal documents. The escrow officer plays a crucial role in coordinating the closing process and ensuring a smooth transaction.

- Earnest Money Deposit: As part of the sales contract, the buyer typically provides an earnest money deposit to demonstrate their seriousness and commitment to the transaction. The earnest money is held in escrow and will be applied towards the purchase price at closing. In the event that the transaction falls through due to a specified contingency, such as a failed inspection, the earnest money may be returned to the buyer.

- Title Search and Title Insurance: During the escrow process, a title search is conducted to ensure that the property's title is clear and free of any liens, encumbrances, or ownership disputes. Title insurance is also obtained to protect the buyer and lender against any unforeseen issues or claims related to the title. The escrow officer coordinates with the title company to ensure that the necessary title work is completed.

- Contingency Removal: Contingencies stated in the sales contract, such as the buyer's ability to obtain financing or the satisfactory completion of inspections, must be addressed within specified timeframes. Once the contingencies are satisfied, the buyer typically provides written confirmation to the seller, removing the contingencies and moving the transaction closer to closing.

- Home Inspections and Repairs: If the sales contract includes an inspection contingency, the buyer may conduct a professional home inspection. Based on the inspection report, the buyer may request repairs or credits from the seller to address any identified issues. Negotiations may occur to determine which repairs will be completed, who will bear the associated costs, and whether any adjustments will be made to the purchase price.

- Final Walk-Through: Prior to closing, the buyer typically conducts a final walk-through of the property to ensure that it is in the agreed-upon condition and that any agreed-upon repairs or improvements have been completed satisfactorily. The final walk-through allows the buyer to confirm that the property is ready for possession.

- Closing Documents and Funds: As the closing date approaches, the escrow officer prepares the necessary closing documents, including the settlement statement, loan documents (if applicable), and any additional legal paperwork required. The parties involved in the transaction, including the buyer, seller, and their respective agents, meet to sign the documents. The buyer provides the remaining funds needed to complete the purchase, including the down payment and closing costs.

- Recording and Disbursement: After all documents are signed and funds are received, the escrow officer oversees the recording of the deed and other necessary documents with the appropriate government agency.

Understanding the sales contract and the escrow process is crucial for a successful closing. By familiarizing yourself with these processes and working closely with the escrow officer and your real estate agent, you can navigate the final stage of the transaction and ensure a smooth and successful sale of your home.

MANAGING HOME INSPECTIONS AND REPAIRS

Home inspections play a vital role in the home selling process, as they provide buyers with a comprehensive assessment of the property's condition. Once the inspection is complete, buyers may request repairs or credits based on the inspection report. Managing these inspections and subsequent repairs requires effective communication, negotiation skills, and attention to detail. In this chapter, we will explore strategies for successfully managing home inspections and repairs:

- Schedule a Pre-Listing Inspection: Consider conducting a pre-listing inspection before listing your home on the market. This allows you to identify potential issues in advance and address them proactively. By addressing any major concerns or making necessary repairs beforehand, you can enhance the overall condition of your home and potentially minimize the number of repair requests during the buyer's inspection.

- Choose a Qualified Home Inspector: Select a qualified and reputable home inspector to conduct the buyer's inspection. Ask for recommendations from your real estate agent or seek referrals from trusted sources. A qualified inspector will thoroughly assess the property, identify any issues, and provide an objective report.

- Be Present During the Inspection: Whenever possible, be present during the buyer's inspection. This allows you to gain firsthand knowledge of the inspector's findings and ask questions. It also demonstrates your commitment to transparency and provides an opportunity to address any concerns raised by the buyer or inspector.

- Review the Inspection Report: Once the inspection is complete, carefully review the inspection report. Understand the inspector's findings, paying attention to any major issues or safety concerns. This will help you assess the scope of necessary repairs or potential negotiation points.

- Consult with Professionals: Seek advice from professionals, such as contractors, repair specialists, or your real estate agent, to better understand the severity and cost of repairs. Their expertise can help you prioritize repairs and determine which ones are essential for addressing safety or structural concerns.

- Assess Reasonable Repair Requests: Buyers may request repairs based on the inspection report. Evaluate each repair request objectively and determine whether it is reasonable and justifiable. Focus on addressing issues that pose safety risks, affect the functionality of the property, or impact compliance with local building codes.

- Obtain Multiple Repair Quotes: For repairs that you agree to address, consider obtaining multiple quotes from reputable contractors. This allows you to compare prices and ensure you are receiving fair estimates. Keep a record of the repair quotes and share them with the buyer to demonstrate your commitment to resolving the issues.

- Negotiate Repair Credits: Instead of completing repairs, buyers may prefer to receive a credit or reduction in the purchase price to address the identified issues. Negotiate in good faith, considering the costs of the repairs and the buyer's request. Keep in mind that offering repair credits can simplify the process and allow the buyer to address the repairs to their satisfaction.

- Document Repairs: If you agree to complete repairs, document the process thoroughly. Retain copies of invoices, receipts, and any warranties associated with the repairs. This documentation provides transparency and reassurance to the buyer that the repairs were completed professionally.

- Request Verification of Repairs: Before the closing, request verification of completed repairs from the contractors or service providers. This ensures that the repairs have been addressed according to the buyer's expectations and the terms agreed upon in the sales contract.

Effective management of home inspections and repairs is crucial for a smooth closing process. By being proactive, understanding the inspection report, evaluating repair requests, negotiating in good faith, and documenting the repair process, you can successfully navigate this stage of the transaction and instill confidence in the buyer. Collaborating with professionals and relying on the guidance of your real estate agent will also contribute to a successful resolution of home inspections and repairs.

NAVIGATING APPRAISALS: ENSURING A FAIR VALUATION

The appraisal process is a critical step in the home selling process, as it determines the fair market value of your property. The appraised value has a significant impact on the buyer's financing options and ultimately affects the successful completion of the sale. Navigating the appraisal process requires understanding the factors involved and taking proactive steps to ensure a fair valuation. In this chapter, we will explore strategies for successfully navigating appraisals:

- Understand the Appraisal Process: Familiarize yourself with the appraisal process to better understand how the value of your property is determined. Appraisers consider factors such as the property's location, size, condition, recent sales of comparable properties, and market trends. By understanding the appraisal methodology, you can better prepare for the valuation process.

- Prepare Your Home for Appraisal: Make sure your home is well-maintained and presents its best possible condition during the appraisal. Clean and declutter the property, repair any noticeable issues, and enhance its curb appeal. Provide the appraiser with a list of recent upgrades, renovations, or improvements you have made to the property. Highlighting these enhancements can positively impact the appraised value.

- Provide Appraiser with Information: Offer the appraiser relevant information about your property, such as unique features, recent comparable sales in the area, or any other factors that could influence the value. Be open and transparent about your property's strengths and improvements, but avoid pressuring or influencing the appraiser to reach a specific value.

- Research Comparable Sales: Conduct your own research on recent comparable sales in your area to gain a better understanding of market trends and property values. Look for properties that are similar in size, location, and condition to yours. This knowledge will help you evaluate the accuracy of the appraiser's valuation and provide supporting evidence if there are discrepancies.

- Accompany the Appraiser: If possible, be present during the appraisal to answer any questions the appraiser may have and provide additional context about the property. Your presence can ensure that important features or recent improvements are not overlooked during the valuation process.

- Review the Appraisal Report: Once the appraisal is complete, carefully review the appraisal report. Ensure that all relevant information about your property has been accurately documented. Pay attention to any discrepancies or errors that may impact the valuation. If you believe there are significant errors, consult with your real estate agent or consider requesting a reassessment.

- Address Appraisal Challenges: In the event that the appraised value falls below the agreed-upon purchase price, you may face appraisal challenges. Consult with your real estate agent to determine the best course of action. Options may include renegotiating the purchase price, providing additional supporting documentation to the appraiser, or requesting a second appraisal if you believe the initial valuation was inaccurate.

- Stay Informed of Market Conditions: Keep abreast of current market conditions and any significant changes that may impact property values in your area. Understanding market trends will help you anticipate potential appraisal challenges and make informed decisions throughout the selling process.

- Maintain Realistic Expectations: While you may have a certain value in mind for your property, it is essential to maintain realistic expectations based on market conditions and recent comparable sales. Remember that the appraiser's role is to provide an objective and impartial valuation based on established criteria.

Navigating the appraisal process requires proactive preparation, open communication, and a realistic understanding of market conditions. By taking steps to prepare your home, providing relevant information to the appraiser, reviewing the appraisal report carefully, and addressing any appraisal challenges that arise, you can increase the likelihood of a fair valuation for your property.

DEALING WITH CONTINGENCIES AND CONTRACT CONDITIONS

Contingencies and contract conditions are an integral part of the home selling process, as they provide protection and flexibility for both buyers and sellers. Contingencies are conditions that must be met for the sale to proceed, while contract conditions outline specific obligations and timelines. Managing contingencies and contract conditions effectively requires clear communication, proactive planning, and timely execution. In this chapter, we will explore strategies for successfully dealing with contingencies and contract conditions:

- Understand Contingencies and Contract Conditions: Familiarize yourself with the various contingencies and contract conditions typically included in a sales contract. Common contingencies include financing, home inspection, appraisal, and sale of the buyer's existing home. Contract conditions may encompass specific timelines for property disclosures, repairs, or other agreed-upon actions.

- Review the Sales Contract: Carefully review the sales contract to identify all contingencies and contract conditions. Ensure that you fully understand the implications and requirements of each provision. Seek clarification from your real estate agent or attorney if you have any questions or concerns.

- Communicate Expectations: Maintain open and clear communication with the buyer and their agent regarding contingencies and contract conditions. Establish mutual understanding and expectations from the beginning to minimize misunderstandings or potential conflicts.

- Establish Realistic Timelines: Work with your real estate agent to establish realistic timelines for fulfilling contingencies and contract conditions. Ensure that the timelines align with your goals and allow sufficient time for necessary actions to be completed. Stay proactive in monitoring and adhering to these timelines.

- Coordinate with Professionals: Collaborate with professionals, such as lenders, inspectors, contractors, and attorneys, to ensure a smooth process in meeting contingencies and contract conditions. Maintain regular communication with these professionals to address any issues or delays promptly.

- Provide Required Disclosures: Fulfill your obligation to provide required disclosures within the specified timeframe. These disclosures may include property condition reports, homeowner association documents, and any other relevant information that you are required to disclose by law.

- Address Home Inspection Findings: If the sales contract includes a home inspection contingency, carefully review the inspection report and promptly address any issues raised by the buyer. Engage with qualified contractors or service providers to evaluate and address necessary repairs or remediation.

- Negotiate Repairs or Credits: In the event that repairs are requested as part of the home inspection contingency, engage in good-faith negotiations with the buyer. Consider the cost, feasibility, and impact of requested repairs, and be willing to find mutually acceptable solutions. Alternatively, you may offer credits or adjustments to the purchase price to address the identified issues.

- Cooperate with Appraisal Process: If an appraisal contingency is included in the sales contract, cooperate with the appraiser and provide any necessary information to support the valuation process. Be prepared for potential challenges and work with your real estate agent to address any discrepancies between the appraised value and the agreed-upon purchase price.

- Stay Proactive and Document Actions: Maintain a proactive approach in meeting contingencies and contract conditions. Document all actions taken and retain copies of relevant documents, including repair receipts, inspection reports, and communication exchanges with the buyer and professionals involved. This documentation ensures transparency and accountability throughout the process.

Successfully managing contingencies and contract conditions requires proactive planning, effective communication, and collaboration with professionals. By understanding the provisions of the sales contract, establishing realistic timelines, promptly addressing issues, and maintaining open communication, you can navigate contingencies and contract conditions smoothly and increase the likelihood of a successful closing.

ASSESSING MARKET CONDITIONS: TIMING THE SALE FOR OPTIMAL RESULTS

The timing of your home sale can significantly impact its success and ultimate selling price. Assessing market conditions and strategically choosing the right time to list your home can maximize your chances of attracting qualified buyers and achieving favorable outcomes. In this chapter, we will explore strategies for assessing market conditions and timing your sale for optimal results:

- Research Local Market Trends: Stay informed about the local real estate market by monitoring trends and analyzing recent sales data. Look for patterns in pricing, inventory levels, and average time on the market. Keep an eye on factors such as seasonality, economic indicators, and interest rates that can influence buyer demand.

- Consult with a Real Estate Agent: Engage the expertise of a knowledgeable real estate agent who has a deep understanding of your local market. A skilled agent can provide valuable insights into current market conditions, pricing strategies, and buyer preferences. Collaborate with your agent to develop a comprehensive marketing plan that aligns with the current market dynamics.

- Analyze Supply and Demand: Evaluate the supply and demand dynamics in your area. Assess the number of homes for sale versus the number of active buyers. A limited supply with high demand can create a favorable selling environment, potentially leading to multiple offers and competitive bidding.

- Consider Seasonal Patterns: Recognize that real estate markets can exhibit seasonal patterns. In some areas, spring and summer months may be more active, while winter months may experience a slowdown. However, this can vary depending on location. Discuss with your agent how these patterns apply to your specific market and consider listing your home during peak buyer activity periods.

- Assess Economic Factors: Keep an eye on economic factors that can influence the real estate market. Factors such as employment rates, wage growth, and interest rates can impact buyer confidence and purchasing power. Favorable economic conditions can create a more robust market, increasing the likelihood of achieving a successful sale.

- Monitor Competing Listings: Pay attention to other listings in your area that are similar to your property. Track their pricing, time on the market, and any changes in listing status. Understanding the competition can help you set a competitive price and position your home effectively in the market.

- Evaluate Buyer Behavior: Gain insights into buyer behavior by observing the volume and characteristics of buyer inquiries in your area. Are there more first-time buyers or investors? Are there specific features or amenities that are particularly desirable? Understanding buyer preferences can inform your marketing strategy and help you highlight your home's unique selling points.

- Plan Ahead: Take into account your personal circumstances and goals when timing your sale. Consider factors such as job relocations, family transitions, and financial considerations. Plan ahead to allow sufficient time for preparations, such as repairs, staging, and marketing efforts.

- Flexibility in Pricing and Negotiation: Be prepared to adapt your pricing and negotiation strategies based on market feedback and buyer response. If the market conditions change or if you receive feedback on the price, remain open to adjusting your listing price or considering offers that align with current market expectations.

- Collaborate with Your Real Estate Agent: Throughout the process, maintain open communication and collaboration with your real estate agent. Regularly review market updates, discuss pricing strategies, and assess the effectiveness of your marketing efforts. Your agent's expertise and guidance can help you make informed decisions and navigate market fluctuations.

Timing your home sale for optimal results requires careful evaluation of market conditions and strategic planning. By researching market trends, consulting with a real estate agent, analyzing supply and demand, and considering economic factors, you can position your home to attract qualified buyers and achieve a successful sale. Adapt your strategies as needed, and maintain open communication with your agent to ensure a well-timed and successful transaction.

PRICING ADJUSTMENTS AND MARKET TRENDS

Pricing your home correctly is crucial for attracting potential buyers and ensuring a successful sale. However, market conditions can shift, and it may be necessary to make pricing adjustments to remain competitive and align with current trends. Understanding market trends and knowing when to make pricing adjustments are key factors in maximizing your chances of a timely and favorable sale. In this chapter, we will explore strategies for assessing market trends and making pricing adjustments:

- Monitor Local Market Conditions: Stay informed about the local real estate market by regularly monitoring market conditions, including inventory levels, median sale prices, and average time on the market. Pay attention to trends such as increasing or decreasing home prices and changes in buyer demand. This information will help you gauge the overall health of the market and make informed pricing decisions.

- Analyze Comparable Sales: Assess recent comparable sales in your area to understand the pricing trends and the value of properties similar to yours. Look for homes that are similar in size, location, condition, and amenities. Analyzing the sale prices of these comparable properties will provide valuable insights into the current market value and guide your pricing strategy.

- Adjust Pricing Strategically: If your home has been on the market for an extended period without attracting substantial interest or offers, it may be necessary to consider a pricing adjustment. Work closely with your real estate agent to evaluate the market feedback and adjust your price strategically. The adjustment should reflect the current market conditions and align with the value of your property.

- Consider Price Range and Competition: Assess the price range of homes in your area that are similar to yours. Determine where your home falls within that range and consider the competition. If your home is at the higher end of the price range and comparable homes are selling at a lower price point, it may be necessary to make a pricing adjustment to stay competitive.

- Evaluate Buyer Feedback: Listen to the feedback provided by potential buyers and their agents. If you consistently receive feedback about the price being too high, it may indicate that a pricing adjustment is necessary. Buyer feedback can provide valuable insights into how your home is perceived in the market and guide your decision-making process.

- Timing of Pricing Adjustments: Consider the timing of your pricing adjustments. If market conditions are shifting and there is an increased supply of homes for sale, making an early pricing adjustment may help your home stand out among the competition. Conversely, if demand is strong and inventory is low, you may have more flexibility in pricing.

- Collaborate with Your Real Estate Agent: Work closely with your real estate agent throughout the process of making pricing adjustments. Leverage their expertise and market knowledge to assess market trends, evaluate feedback, and determine the appropriate pricing strategy. Your agent can provide valuable guidance and help you navigate the complexities of pricing adjustments.

- Communicate Pricing Adjustments: Effectively communicate any pricing adjustments to potential buyers and their agents. Update your listing with the new price and ensure that all marketing materials, online listings, and advertisements reflect the adjusted price. Clear and transparent communication will help attract renewed interest and showcase your responsiveness to market conditions.

- Be Realistic and Flexible: When making pricing adjustments, it's important to be realistic and flexible. Consider the market trends, feedback, and comparable sales data to determine an appropriate price range. By being open to adjusting your price strategically, you increase your chances of attracting motivated buyers and securing a timely sale.

- Evaluate the Impact of Pricing Adjustments: Monitor the impact of pricing adjustments on buyer interest and activity. Track the number of inquiries, showings, and offers received after the adjustment. Evaluate whether the adjustment has generated renewed interest and increased buyer engagement. If necessary, be prepared to make additional adjustments to ensure your pricing remains competitive.

Pricing adjustments and market trends are crucial considerations when selling a home. Monitoring local market conditions, analyzing comparable sales, and evaluating buyer feedback help sellers make informed pricing decisions. Strategic adjustments to the listing price may be necessary to remain competitive and attract potential buyers. Collaboration with a real estate agent and timely communication of pricing adjustments are vital. Sellers must be realistic, flexible, and responsive to market trends to maximize their chances of a successful sale. Regular evaluation of the impact of pricing adjustments ensures that the listing remains competitive and attracts motivated buyers.

SELLING IN A COMPETITIVE MARKET: STANDING OUT FROM THE COMPETITION

In a competitive real estate market, it's essential to find ways to make your home stand out and attract potential buyers. With multiple properties available for sale, distinguishing your home from the competition becomes crucial for a successful sale. This chapter explores effective strategies to help you stand out in a competitive market:

- Enhance Curb Appeal: First impressions matter. Boost your home's curb appeal by ensuring the exterior is well-maintained, landscaping is tidy, and the entryway is inviting. Consider adding fresh paint, updating the front door, or adding decorative touches to make your home visually appealing from the moment potential buyers arrive.

- Stage for Success: Proper staging can transform your home and make it more appealing to buyers. Clear out clutter, rearrange furniture for optimal flow, and consider adding tasteful decor and neutral colors to create an inviting and aspirational ambiance. Professional staging services can be worth considering for maximizing the impact.

- High-Quality Listing Photos: Invest in professional photography to capture your home's best features. High-quality, well-lit, and properly framed photos can make a significant difference in attracting potential buyers online. Utilize visually engaging images to highlight your home's unique selling points and create a lasting impression.

- Engaging Property Descriptions: Craft compelling property descriptions that highlight the key features and benefits of your home. Showcase its unique characteristics, such as architectural details, recent renovations, or energy-efficient upgrades. Use descriptive language to create an emotional connection and pique buyers' interest.

- Leverage Online Marketing: Make the most of online platforms to market your home effectively. Utilize multiple listing services, social media platforms, and real estate websites to showcase your property to a wide audience. Consider creating virtual tours or video walkthroughs to provide a more immersive experience for potential buyers.

- Targeted Marketing Campaigns: Develop targeted marketing campaigns to reach specific buyer demographics or niches. Identify potential buyer profiles for your property and tailor your marketing messages accordingly. This may include focusing on families, young professionals, or downsizers, depending on the unique features and location of your home.

- Highlight Unique Selling Points: Identify and emphasize the unique selling points of your home. Whether it's a stunning view, a spacious backyard, or high-end finishes, focus on these aspects in your marketing materials and conversations with potential buyers. Differentiate your property by showcasing what makes it truly special.

- Competitive Pricing: Set a competitive price for your home based on market conditions, recent sales data, and the advice of your real estate agent. A well-priced property will attract more attention from buyers and increase the chances of receiving competitive offers. Avoid overpricing, as it may deter potential buyers and prolong the selling process.

- Flexibility in Showings and Negotiations: Be flexible with showing schedules and open houses to accommodate potential buyers' needs. Respond promptly to inquiries, showing requests, and offers to demonstrate your commitment to a smooth and efficient transaction. Flexibility in negotiations can also help secure a favorable deal.

- Collaborate with a Skilled Real Estate Agent: Work closely with a knowledgeable and experienced real estate agent who understands the local market dynamics and has a track record of success. Their expertise, guidance, and negotiation skills will be instrumental in helping you navigate a competitive market and stand out from the competition.

By implementing these strategies, you can position your home as an attractive option in a competitive market. Enhancing its appeal, utilizing effective marketing techniques, and working collaboratively with your real estate agent will increase your chances of selling your home quickly and at a favorable price.

OPEN HOUSES AND SHOWINGS: CREATING AN INVITING EXPERIENCE

Open houses and showings are key opportunities to showcase your home to potential buyers and make a lasting impression. Creating an inviting and memorable experience for visitors can significantly impact their perception of your property and increase the likelihood of receiving competitive offers. In this chapter, we will explore strategies for creating an inviting experience during open houses and showings:

- Clean and Declutter: Prior to any showing or open house, thoroughly clean and declutter your home. A clean and organized space not only creates a positive impression but also allows potential buyers to envision themselves living in the home. Pay attention to details such as freshening up the bathrooms, tidying up personal items, and ensuring all rooms are presentable.

- Maximize Natural Light: Open curtains and blinds to let in natural light, as it can create a warm and welcoming atmosphere. Bright and well-lit spaces tend to appear more inviting and spacious. Consider removing heavy drapes or furniture that may block natural light from entering the rooms.

- Create a Neutral Ambiance: Use neutral colors and decor to create a welcoming ambiance that appeals to a wide range of potential buyers. Neutral tones on the walls, furniture, and accessories can help create a blank canvas, allowing visitors to envision their own personal style in the space.

- Stage for Maximum Appeal: Consider professional staging services or work with your real estate agent to arrange furniture and decor in a way that highlights the home's best features. Well-placed furniture and strategic decor can enhance the flow of the space and create an appealing visual narrative for visitors.

- Pleasant Scents and Fresh Air: Pleasant scents can have a positive impact on visitors' perception of your home. Consider using subtle air fresheners, scented candles, or fresh flowers to create an inviting aroma. Additionally, ensure there is proper ventilation to keep the air fresh and minimize any potential odors.

- Enhance Curb Appeal: Pay attention to the exterior of your home to make a strong first impression. Maintain a well-manicured lawn, trim hedges, and add potted plants or flowers near the entrance.

Clear any clutter, such as toys or gardening equipment, from the yard or front porch. A visually appealing exterior sets the stage for a positive experience.

- Create Welcoming Spaces: Stage key areas of the home, such as the living room, kitchen, and master bedroom, to create inviting spaces that showcase their potential. Arrange furniture to highlight functionality and flow, add tasteful decor to create warmth, and use soft lighting to create a cozy ambiance.

- Provide Information: Prepare informational materials, such as brochures or fact sheets, that highlight the key features and amenities of your home. Include details about recent renovations, upgrades, or unique selling points. Visitors can take these materials with them for future reference, helping them remember the highlights of your home.

- Offer Refreshments: Consider providing light refreshments during open houses, such as water, coffee, or cookies. This small gesture can create a welcoming atmosphere and encourage visitors to spend more time exploring your home.

- Give Space and Privacy: During showings and open houses, allow potential buyers to explore the home at their own pace. Offer guidance and answer questions, but also give them privacy to discuss their thoughts and envision themselves living in the space.

By implementing these strategies, you can create an inviting and memorable experience for visitors during open houses and showings. A well-presented and welcoming environment can leave a positive impression on potential buyers and increase the likelihood of receiving competitive offers for your home. Collaborating with your real estate agent to optimize the showing experience will further enhance your chances of a successful sale.

UNDERSTANDING TAX IMPLICATIONS AND CAPITAL GAINS

When selling a home, it's important to be aware of the tax implications and potential capital gains that may arise from the sale. Having a clear understanding of these factors can help you plan accordingly and make informed decisions throughout the selling process. In this chapter, we will explore key considerations related to tax implications and capital gains:

- Primary Residence Exemption: In many states, homeowners may be eligible for a primary residence exemption, also known as the principal residence exemption, which allows them to exclude a portion or all of the capital gains from the sale of their primary residence from taxation. Check the specific rules and regulations in your state or region to determine if you qualify for this exemption.

- Ownership and Occupancy Requirements: To qualify for the primary residence exemption, certain ownership and occupancy requirements must typically be met. These requirements may include the minimum period of ownership and the duration of time the property was used as the primary residence. Consult with a tax professional or refer to relevant tax laws to ensure you meet these requirements.

- Capital Gains Calculation: If the sale of your home does not qualify for the primary residence exemption or if the capital gains exceed the exempted amount, you may be subject to capital gains tax. Capital gains are generally calculated by subtracting the property's adjusted basis (purchase price plus qualified improvements and minus depreciation) from the selling price.

- Consult with a Tax Professional: Tax laws can be complex and vary based on jurisdiction. Consulting with a tax professional or accountant who specializes in real estate transactions can provide valuable guidance tailored to your specific situation. They can help you understand the tax implications, calculate potential capital gains, and explore any available deductions or exemptions.

- Keep Track of Home Improvements: Maintain detailed records of any home improvements or renovations you have made over the years. This includes receipts, invoices, and other documentation. Qualified improvements can increase the adjusted basis of your home, potentially reducing the capital gains tax liability.

- 1031 Exchange: In some countries, a 1031 exchange, also known as a like-kind exchange, allows sellers to defer capital gains taxes by reinvesting the proceeds from the sale into a similar property within a specific timeframe. This option is subject to certain rules and restrictions, so consult with a tax professional to determine if it's applicable in your situation.

- State and Local Taxes: Consider state and local tax implications that may apply in addition to federal taxes. Some jurisdictions impose their own capital gains tax or have specific rules regarding real estate transactions. Be aware of these additional tax obligations and seek professional advice to ensure compliance.

- Plan Ahead: It's wise to consider tax implications and capital gains early in the home selling process. By understanding potential tax liabilities, you can make informed decisions about pricing, timing, and potential deductions. This early planning can help you maximize your financial outcome and minimize any unexpected tax obligations.

- Stay Updated on Tax Laws: Tax laws and regulations can change over time. Stay informed about any updates or amendments to tax laws that may impact your real estate transactions. This will ensure you have the most accurate and up-to-date information when making decisions related to tax implications and capital gains.

- Seek Professional Advice: Ultimately, seeking professional advice from a tax professional or accountant is highly recommended. They can provide personalized guidance based on your specific circumstances, help you navigate complex tax laws, and ensure compliance with relevant regulations.

Understanding the tax implications and potential capital gains associated with selling your home is essential for effective financial planning. By staying informed, seeking professional advice, and maintaining accurate records, you can make informed decisions and optimize your financial outcome when selling your home.

POST-SALE CONSIDERATIONS: MOVING, RELOCATION, AND CLOSING OUT THE TRANSACTION

Once the sale of your home is complete, there are important post-sale considerations to address. These include planning your move, managing relocation logistics, and ensuring a smooth closing of the transaction. In this chapter, we will explore key considerations for this phase:

- Moving Logistics: Develop a comprehensive moving plan to ensure a smooth transition to your new location. This may involve hiring professional movers, obtaining packing supplies, and coordinating the logistics of transporting your belongings. Create a timeline and checklist to stay organized and minimize stress during the moving process.

- Change of Address: Notify relevant parties of your change of address, including the post office, utility companies, financial institutions, and government agencies. Update your address with subscriptions, online accounts, and any other entities that require your current contact information. This ensures that important mail and communications are redirected appropriately.

- Relocation Assistance: If you are relocating to a new area, consider seeking assistance from relocation services or your new employer. These services can provide valuable support, such as assisting with housing arrangements, school enrollment, and acclimating to your new community. Take advantage of resources available to ease the transition.

- Closing Out the Transaction: Ensure that all necessary paperwork and financial matters are completed to close out the transaction. Coordinate with your real estate agent, attorney, and any other involved parties to ensure a smooth closing process. Review and sign all required documents, and follow up to ensure that funds are transferred and the transaction is officially closed.

- Property Handover: If applicable, coordinate the handover of keys, access codes, and any other property-related items to the new owner. Ensure that all agreed-upon repairs, fixtures, or items are left in the condition specified in the sales contract. Complete a final walkthrough to verify the property's condition and address any outstanding issues.

- Financial Considerations: Evaluate the financial implications of the sale. Consult with a financial advisor to discuss potential tax implications, investment opportunities, and strategies for managing the proceeds from the sale. Plan accordingly to make the most of your financial resources and address any tax obligations in a timely manner.

- Homeowner Association and Community Obligations: If you were part of a homeowner association or community with ongoing obligations, ensure that all necessary paperwork and payments are completed. Notify the appropriate entities of your departure and update them with your new contact information. Understand any obligations or procedures for transferring membership or resolving outstanding matters.

- Settling into Your New Home: Take the time to settle into your new home and familiarize yourself with the new surroundings. Unpack and organize your belongings, set up utilities and services, and make any necessary adjustments or improvements to create a comfortable living environment. Explore the community, meet neighbors, and get involved in local activities to establish a sense of belonging.

- Preserve Important Documents: Safely store and preserve all relevant documents related to the sale, including the sales contract, disclosures, inspection reports, and closing statements. These documents may be important for future reference, tax purposes, or any potential legal matters. Keep digital and physical copies in a secure location.

- Reflect and Celebrate: Take a moment to reflect on your home-selling journey and celebrate the successful sale of your property. Recognize the efforts and hard work you invested, and embrace the new opportunities and possibilities that lie ahead. Allow yourself to celebrate this significant milestone.

Addressing post-sale considerations ensures a seamless transition and closure of the home selling process. By planning your move, managing relocation logistics, completing necessary paperwork, and settling into your new home, you can successfully close out the transaction and embark on the next chapter of your life.

www.ingramcontent.com/pod-product-compliance
Lightning Source LLC
Chambersburg PA
CBHW070649220526
45466CB00001B/353